Title of book: Rising Eagle

Author's name: Geduld Veldsman

ISBN: 978-0-620-92600-3

Front cover images by Lian-Robert Jack

First printing edition 2021

Contents

Acknowledgements

This book is based on the highs and lows of my personal life journey with God on my side. I am grateful for a number of people in my life who encouraged me to start writing my story and persevere with it, until it could be published.

I thank my brother Kaizer Veldsman for taking me to school when I was in primary school. He made sure a received an education.

I thank my teacher at Newton Primary School, Mr Thomas Matthee, Craig Ledimo, Wayne Arendse, Danielle Michiel, Willie Malgas and the Newton Rugby Club for whom I played in the third team in that time due to my age.

I thank Sidney Cupido, Rachel Thomas, Samuel Thomas, Wesley Goetham who took me in as one of their children. To Gert and Catherine Warries I am grateful. For my spiritual leaders, Evangelist Karel De Bruyn, Apostle De Bruyn, Evangelist Mario Jonathan Appollis, Monica Appollis and Morne Swarts.

A special word of gratitude is due to Elisabeth and Frank Loose, Marc and Carol Morilly and Len Moses, who never stopped supporting me during my high school and student years and for showing their confidence in me and for all their patience and help.

I am also grateful to Christiaan and Rosy Beyers and James and Linda Willemse for opening their doors to me during my time in Bonnievale. I thank Bonnievale United for always believing in my leadership abilities.

I would like to acknowledge with gratitude the support and love of my cousin Robert Titus, Dr Demore Pretorius, advocate Willem Small, my brother and sister, Theo and Annelie, my wife, Anelia Veldsman, Christopher Petersen and all my family members. They kept me going, going, and going. This book would not have been possible without them.

Finally, to my mother. There would be no Geduld Veldsman without you giving birth to me.

So much gratitude, love and grace to all of you.

Foreword

I was expecting to see a shy boy when I called him to my classroom. However, a brave young boy with a broad smile stepped into my classroom. Geduld entered my classroom with enough confidence that left a lasting impression. He had no idea why I wanted to see him, but that did not prevent him from introducing himself to me with great boldness. It was the beginning of a good friendship that developed between Geduld and me.

I did not know him at all. I only heard about the cute, well-mannered boy who did not have it so easy in life. All the educators were very impressed with this beautiful boy and spoke of him with praise. After exchanging a few words with him, I understood why.

This encounter with Geduld took place at the beginning of his Grade 10 year. I immediately realised that this boy was going to get far in life. He just had that something extra and special in him that set him apart from other learners at school.

In his Grade 12 year, Geduld was elected as the head boy of Weltevrede Secondary. He always joked that he made history at Weltevrede as he was the oldest head boy the school has ever had. He was 22 years old in his matric year.

The following sayings are well known to many of us: "Do not become a product of your circumstances," and: "Rise above your circumstances." These two sayings form Geduld's journey from yesterday to today ... his flight from low to high. Circumstances never held him back from what he wanted to be and reach in life.

A small, humble farm boy who moved mountains and whose horizons broadened so much. The prayer of Jabez came true in Geduld Veldsman's life. God enlarged his territory and blessed him infinitely.

Geduld's broad smile is what immediately strikes you when you meet him. His humble nature and down-to-earth personality are two characteristics that immediately stand out to you. And if you can look pass his broad smile, you will often find that Geduld stands in front of you with bare feet. His love for walking barefoot is known to all who know and love him.

Self-confidence is a trait that Geduld has received in excess. Being afraid or afraid of new challenges is not in his frame of mind. He grabs the proverbial bull by the horns and strives to always be positive and successful.

"Vlieg soos 'n arend" is a famous Afrikaans gospel song. An eagle has many characteristics that make it an absolutely unique bird species. And when I think of Geduld Veldsman, I think of an eagle. Geduld soared like an eagle because God's love carried him.

Carol Morilly

Foreword

I am delighted to write this foreword, not only because Geduld Veldsman has been a student of mine but also because I deeply believe in the educative value this book could have on the lives of many South African boys and girls going through similar circumstances, especially here in democratic South Africa.

I also believe that teachers, at any stage of their career, can enrich and strengthen their teaching by recognising students with potential and encouraging them to become the best they can be. When teachers work they create the potential for change in search of fulfilment. They do this by taking their students into the unknown to shape what is coming.

When I first met this 16-year-old boy in 2000, he was in Grade 7. I did not know what to expect. I started to encourage my class with slogans such as: "Winners never give up." "Winners are not afraid to make mistakes." And: "Every day winners do what needs to be done."

Geduld was the first to make these slogans his own. He tried very hard to live by them.

In sharing his experiences and tribulations in this book and by telling us about the people who influenced him and pushed him to be who he is today, Geduld Veldsman also tells us who we are. Thus his words inspire in all of us the passion to not give up, but to take action, to make an impact, to find our purpose, to help others and to move forward to the mutual goal of shaping the world.

TJ Matthee

Introduction

We can either live life with the intent to impress people or to have an impact on people. An impression lasts but for a brief moment, but an impact can have an everlasting effect on a person's life.

This book will doubtlessly impact many people's lives. It also has the potential to turn around a life that has been badly affected by negative, traumatic or terrible life experiences. This thought really provokes me and makes me so grateful that I was chosen to play a role in this life-changing project. I earnestly look forward to hear testimonies on how this book has changed precious lives.

In this story we can clearly see that *grace* is indeed an amazing thing. We all desperately need more grace to make the most of our lives here on earth. We have only one life to live. May God's grace empower us to give life our very best shot. By the grace of God, Geduld has indeed given life has very best shot. And this will have a ripple effect on many people's lives.

I feel so inspired to do my very best each day of my life since I read Geduld's life story. In his story we can clearly see how God has changed and transformed a hopeless and poor boy into a powerful *force for good*. Yes, this is what Geduld has become!

To make the most of our lives, we should grow. We should do our very best to grow through whatever we go through in life, no matter what. It is not enough to just *go* through stuff. We should *grow* through stuff. Moreover, we should learn each lesson that is locked up or hidden in every situation, circumstance or event. Always be mindful that there is something positive in every negative situation.

Both a negative and a positive cannot stand on its own. The truth is, it takes a positive and a negative to switch on a light. You are in the dark if you only see the negative in your situation or circumstances. Believe me, it is easy to see only the negative for it screams at us. Moreover, it is easier to become negative than to stay positive. We should search really hard to see the positive in life, but don't stop until you discover the positive. Then build upon it until your situation turns around in a positive direction.

This is how you give life your best shot. You should also study your daily routine. An unexamined life is not worth living. Look at your daily activities and ask yourself, which of these activities are senseless? These are activities that are like a car with spinning wheels. It moves, but it is taking you nowhere. You are busy, but your busy-ness is producing no results. We can also call it "non-value activities". These are activities that do not add any value to your life. It does not cause you to grow or develop. You remain the same person, year after year after year. This is so sad.

Also study the people in your life, keeping in mind that we become like the people with whom we spend most of our time. The Good Book says people are like iron; they sharpen and shape one another. This is the power of association.
Do your friends add value to your life? Do they inspire you to grow and to become a better person? This is an important and critical aspect of life. If you walk with the wise, you too will be wise. If you walk with fools, you too will become a

fool. Walk with successful people and you too will be successful. This is how life works.

So let us take some positive action. Identify activities adding value to your life. Make it your goal to add activities like these to your daily routine. Also identify friends that will add positive value to your life. Pursue them and befriend them. Believe me, these two actions will have a very positive effect on you and your life. You will undergo subtle changes and transformations.

In conclusion, apply the principle of *focus*. This principle says, whatever you focus on you empower, and what you empower will control you and your life. So many people are controlled by negativity because they focus on and entertain negativity. If you think negative, you will feel negative and see negative results. The very same thing applies to positivity. As I said, identify value-adding people and activities and then give it your full attention.

Here are some of the advantages of living a *focused* life:

1. A focused mind determines positive outcomes.
2. A focused mind drives performance.
3. A focused mind overcomes weaknesses and challenges.
4. A focused mind accomplishes much.
5. A focused mind ignores distractions.
6. A focused mind is creative and strong.
7. A focused mind keeps the target in sight.
8. A focused mind is selective.

Please invest quality time to ponder on these four powerful thoughts:

- Getting to know yourself on a much deeper level is the key to great success.
- The deeper you travel within through soul searching, the further you can go in life.
- You are born to succeed. Why settle for anything less than success?
- Nothing succeeds like *success*.

See you in Chapter 1.

Chapter 1
Dreams and poverty

Dream the impossible dream, for with God all things are possible.

This is the journey of a young boy who was born in poverty, but poverty and hunger did not stop him from dreaming. So many of us do not take advantage of this wonderful opportunity we have called *dreaming*. We tend to value the things we pay for more than we value the things we get for free in life. Our hearts, mind, imagination, dreams and desires come for free. Use them!

A dream is not from God if you can achieve that dream all by yourself. However, a dream is from God if you cannot make it come true without God. Think about this. God will not do what you can do. God specialises in what seems impossible. This is what makes God the *almighty* God. Allow God to be almighty in your life. You do this by thinking big and by developing your faith. Grow your faith until your faith becomes *unshakeable*.

To dream costs you nothing. However, your dream can eventually become a money-making machine. The world is filled with many wealthy people who were once very poor.

In Ephesians 3:20 the Good Book says God is able to do exceedingly abundantly above all that we could ever ask for, think or imagine and even far beyond our wildest dreams. This verse reveals the four levels of receiving things from God:
1. Pray, which include to ask things from God;
2. Think, for we accomplish what we think about;
3. Imagine, for we can achieve what we can imagine through visualisation; and
4. Dream, for dreams can come true.

Our role in this wonderful advantage we have is to think what we really want, to tap into our imagination through the immense power of visualisation, to dream big dreams and to trust God all the way, until we see the fulfilment of all the desires of our hearts. Remember, desire in Latin means "from the Father". Do not ignore your desires; give them close attention; value them; esteem them; treasure them; honour them. And continually give thanks to God.

The rest is up to God and the universe. God and the universe will lead, guide and direct you to the right people, the right opportunities and the right open doors. Give God and the universe a chance in your life. Also develop a sensitivity to your intuition for leadership and guidance. Intuition is thoughts without thinking. Don't take these thoughts lightly.

Moreover, continually practice hope, faith, patience, self-discipline, responsibility and childlike trust. You will continually grow and develop yourself when you practice these things consistently. In consistency lies the power, and power is the ability to make wonderful things happen.

Don't underestimate the power within you. No one came into this world without power. Your Maker has invested power within you because you cannot succeed in life without power. You were born to *succeed*, not only to survive.

This is what has happened to me over the years. My journey was hard, tough and very difficult. But tough times don't last forever; tough people, however, do. I have lasted and I have now decided to write this book to help many other people to last. For I know and understand the deep pain of suffering and poverty. I know the disappointment of having nothing working in your favour, but many things working against you.

This book is me walking side by side with you as a friend. Please read this book with an open mind and an open heart. Allow me to inspire, motivate, encourage, teach, train, equip and empower you. Both the mind and the heart work like a parachute. It is only functional when it is wide open. Let me be your unseen friend. Who knows, we even might meet in real life someday. The age of technology has made this big world so very small. I know you agree with me. So walk and work with me through all of these pages. And remember, reading is to the mind what exercise is to the body. Moreover, readers eventually becomes leaders. Don't stay a follower!

I am here to help you to become a powerful leader. This world desperately needs more leaders, for followers cannot make positive things happen. Followers wait for other people to help them and to make the changes. Don't be a follower. Only leaders can make positive changes in life.

Can you imagine what would happen if there were more leaders in this desperate world? Far too many leaders collected followers instead of producing more leaders. Now is the time to produce leaders. Someone once said a leader with followers is only a person taking a walk. Don't take walks with followers; change them into leaders.

Together we can turn the negativity in this world into positive outcomes. This resonates with my spirit. In fact, it excites me. You can become one of these Change Agents or Game Changers. I am the living proof that a nobody can become a somebody. My friend, I am confident that you are one of us too.

Please invest quality time to ponder on these four powerful thoughts:

- You have the power to change your circumstances.
- If you want to be strong, learn how to fight alone.
- In life become a fighter, not a quitter.
- For God nothing is impossible.

See you in Chapter 2.

Chapter 2
Primary school

Without vision people will perish.

My dream felt impossible. At that stage of my life I had no clue that the impossible can be done if you have faith in God. Only later I discovered the Bible verse that says all things are possible for those who believe.

These words became seeds in my mind and heart. As these seeds were growing within me, little by little, it created a sense of hope in me. And hope is the pleasant expectation that the best is yet to come. How can things not work out well if you have a positive expectation that the best is yet to come?

Our past does not equal our future. If the good God allows bad and terrible things to happen to us, He also intends to bring good out of those bad things. The Good Book says all things work together for those who love God and are called according to his purpose. God created you for a reason. And you should discover that specific reason.

This positive expectation begin growing stronger and stronger in me. I can say this now, but during the painful days of my youth I was unaware that it was happening to me. Pain has a way of making you blind to positive things. When we focus only on our pain, our pain will make everything seems hopeless and dark.

To be honest, I experienced many dark days and dark nights on my journey. And it really made me unsure whether things would ever worked out for me.

I was born in a family that was very poor. We did not have much to eat. I was the third born, a boy. I did not go to school, and I also did not have a social life. So clearly I remember that at the age of nine, my mother forget me at the train station because she was very drunk. Yes, she forgot about her nine-year-old boy. Sad to say, I was a burden to her. Nonetheless, on an unconscious level her love for me had to be endless. So eventually she realised that she had forgotten her son at the train station.

I later on read in the Good Book that Jesus' family did not miss Him initially when He stayed behind in the temple in Jerusalem. Only later on their journey back home did they realise He was not with them. This really made me feel better.

To be honest, everything was not fun in the Veldsman home. It so happened that I was the only one with the surname of Williams, which was my mother's surname. Everybody saw me as someone else's child because of my surname that was different. I was not sent to school at the right age due to fact that my parents did not know when to send a child to school. No wonder the Good Book says people without knowledge will perish. This really makes me appreciate my education today, as well as all the people who supported me to get a proper education. We all owe a debt of gratitude to the people who have been good to us.

We lived on a small farm in Paarl for many years. Back in those days' people on the farms were uninformed about sending children to school. Everybody lived only for themselves. The word *Ubuntu* was not part of that farming community. I can still remember one day, I was ten, when my older brother told my mother that it is time to send Geduld to school. "Geduld cannot read or write," he said. "What will happen to him when he is older?" She then told my brother to take me to school so that I could learn to read and write.

My brother took me and my birth certificate and off to school we went. I remember that he spoke to the principal. The principal's words were that I was too old for Grade R, but that he would see how far I could fit in with the school structure.

This was the most difficult time in my life since there was no preschool foundation in my life.
How can one build a house without a foundation? Likewise, how can one build a *life* without a foundation? The Good Book asks, What can the righteous do without a foundation?

My first day at school was very challenging and extremely hard for everybody in the class could write their names. Some could even read a few words. It was really very embarrassing and hard for me to sit there, very afraid that the teacher would ask me to read or write my name. Needless to say, I was very insecure, scared and timid.

My first day at school was supposed to be one of my happiest days. However, I felt ashamed for being the oldest kid in the class room that could not even write his own name. The hardest thing for me was when they asked the ages of the children in the class room and everybody was six, but I was ten years old. Everybody laughed at me and made fun of my age. Every time they saw me, they would avoid me for they would not play with the boy so much older than them.

This was really hard. No one showed any interest in me. I was the lonely boy during school breaks. I felt deeply despised and rejected. It was hell on earth for me. Again, only later on I learned that Jesus too was despised and rejected by people. And He went through all of that for my sake.

Today I can look back and say that my teacher was sent by God. She showed me so much understanding, compassion, love, mercy and grace. She really walked the extra mile to ensure that I could master the skills of reading and writing. She invested extra hours in me and gave me the special attention that I so desperately needed at that time.

There is a principle that says anything you give focused attention to will begin to grow and develop. This is what this teacher's special attention did for me. I began to grow and develop, little by little, step by step.

My teacher allowed me to read very slowly during reading time in the class. This teacher really went out of her way to make school enjoyable for me. As I am writing this, I can still feel my heart filling with so much *gratitude* over the critical role that this teacher played in my broken life. Her love and genuine care begin to fix me and heal me. It was evident in the fact that my sense of self-worth and my self-confidence started improving. I began to feel better about myself. She even kindly asked the other children not to make fun of me. I needed this!

From that moment on I decided not to disappoint this teacher, but to make sure that I would pass Grade R and make her proud. And I succeeded. I learned to read and write, and I passed Grade R.

What broke my heart, though, was the fact that my parents were not interested in my positive progress and school results. However, later on I understood that education was not important to my parents since they were uneducated. People cannot give what they do not have. This understanding really brought some closure to me.

My journey onward through life did not become easier. Not at all. Things were still very hard for me because my parents never stopped drinking. They never contributed anything for me to enjoy school, because we were too poor. Most of their money was spent on alcohol and some food on the table. I still remember the times they really tried to stop drinking, but somewhere along the line they would only start all over again. Old habits die hard, the saying goes.

I also recall the time when my father lost his job on the farm and we had to leave the farm. We

ended up living next to the Main Road of Paarl. It was very embarrassing for me for most of my peers and school friends could see where I lived when they drove to school with the school bus. They started mocking me for living next to the road with no food and running water to wash ourselves.

Children can be so cruel. They know nothing about the compassion and love we have to show one another. We only learn these things as we get older. We make these characteristics habits, and then these habits make us.

But I never stopped going to school. Instead, I strived to do my very best at school and gave it my very best shot. God was good to us, because there was always something to eat at home and at school. I deeply appreciated our peanut butter, jam and the big milkshake dessert.

The truth is, we never really are without reasons to give thanks and to be grateful. As I said earlier, it is very easy to see all the negative things in our lives. But we should search real hard for the few positive things. The more we practise

looking for positive things in our lives, the more obvious they will become.

I specifically remember one teacher who gave me a loaf of bread and powdered milk every day to take home after school. This act of kindness kept me positive and motivated me to keep on going to school every day. At the same time it trained me on an unconscious level to be kind to other people. We can either break people down or lift them up. At the least, if you can't help them, don't hurt them.

My entire life journey with its many challenges and the many painful life experiences has indeed moulded, groomed, developed, equipped and empowered me to serve and help other people. Nothing just happens; everything happens for a purpose and a reason. It is our responsibility to discover what the purpose or reason for our suffering was. If we don't discover the reason for our suffering, we will become negative, bitter, hateful and revengeful.

Suffering provides us with valuable life lessons if we are open minded and willing to learn them.

looking for positive things in our lives, the more obvious they will become.

I specifically remember one teacher who gave me a loaf of bread and powdered milk every day to take home after school. This act of kindness kept me positive and motivated me to keep on going to school every day. At the same time it trained me on an unconscious level to be kind to other people. We can either break people down or lift them up. At the least, if you can't help them, don't hurt them.

My entire life journey with its many challenges and the many painful life experiences has indeed moulded, groomed, developed, equipped and empowered me to serve and help other people. Nothing just happens; everything happens for a purpose and a reason. It is our responsibility to discover what the purpose or reason for our suffering was. If we don't discover the reason for our suffering, we will become negative, bitter, hateful and revengeful.

Suffering provides us with valuable life lessons if we are open minded and willing to learn them.

Chapter 3
A new town and school

Have the will to fight and to get up when you fall.

At one stage we lived in a shack in Paarl. Our parents started to drink more and more every day. There were even times when there were no food in our home, only some water to drink from one community tap.

My brothers, some of my friends and I started walking from door to door asking people for food to eat. We had some good days and some bad days. Some people were not so eager to give food to wandering children. Other people were very rude to us for knocking on their doors for food. They felt we were invading their private space.

This only makes sense to me now. And it made me decide to be more kind to suffering kids. The Good Book says God will reward those who pity the poor. And another verse says he who is kind to the poor lends to the Lord, and he will reward him for what he has done.

I remember the day we decided to go to the waste dump in Paarl to see if we could find something good to eat. We decide this because we were scared of the people shouting at us for knocking on their doors to beg for food. I will never forget that I, as a young boy, had to eat from bins and visit the landfills in Paarl to scratch for something proper to eat. Poverty and desperation are best friends. Poor people have no options and it can reduce them to the level of animals. No wonder people are so closed to God's heart. The book of Proverbs speaks a lot about poor people and constantly encourages people to take care of the poor.

Maybe you are thinking now, how on earth can there be anything wholesome to eat at a dump? Well, in our world the saying was beggars can't be choosers. No one is born to be a beggar, but life happens. We also searched for shoes for the winter days. By the grace of God I managed to stay in school with all the drama going on in my life, including a mother and a father who never stopped drinking.

Attending school and the few kind and good-hearted teachers were the only positive things in my life. They were the game changers. Thank God!

I cannot imagine what my life would have been like if there was no positivity to be found anywhere. Those few positive things provided me with some hope and light in my dark world. Negativity is darkness and positivity provides light. This made me realise that God was with me, even though it did not feel like it at that time. I honestly felt deeply alone and abandoned. Loneliness has no place route.

I always had faith that my parents would stop drinking one day. Sadly, that never happened. Never did we receive something new for Christmas or something to celebrate about during the Christmas holidays. Nothing about life seemed to change for the better. Obtaining social grants should have brought about some changes, but instead my parents used the money to support their drinking habits.

I also remember the day I ended up in hospital due to a wound on my head. I lost some blood and had to stay in hospital for a couple of days during the school holidays. Today I still carry the scar on my head of what happened that day.

My family life was not good at all. It was very painful, tough and hard for me. Family should be a place of love, peace, safety and security, especially during one's childhood. I experienced none of these things that were supposed to form the foundation of my life.

We then moved to Wellington to stay with my mother's family. For the very first time I met my cousin and other family members. This was one of the best moments in my life. I was positively impacted to see that we had other family members who were also living in Wellington. Again I learned the lesson that life is never 100% negative or bad.

I also remember we had some pleasant moments in my aunt's caravan in the backyard. We were eight people living in a small caravan, but at least for us that was a home for a few years. I now have so much appreciation for the good things I am able to enjoy in life.

I had so much appreciation for the positive experience of staying in a caravan. And one positive experience can eventually lead to many other positive experiences.

Our lives began changing, a little here and a little there. I think it is very true that we are never really without a reason to be grateful. It is just that the negative things are shouting so loudly for our attention while the positive things happen silently. We have to look carefully to see it. And once you see it, you have to focus on it so that it can increase. Whatever we give attention to tends to grow.

During that year I attended Newton Primary School. The school was not far from home and it was something new and fresh for me. It was another positive life experience to move away from Charlton's Hill Primary School where everybody knew that I was older than all the other kids in my class.

This new school felt like a fresh start and a new beginning. But when I started at Newton Primary in Grade 5 everybody again started to make fun of me because I was older than everybody else in the classroom and my writing skills were not the very best. What made it even harder is the fact that I could not take part in any sport activities due to my age. I had to deal with that. This was another positive life experience I was robbed of, since extramural activities contribute to one's growth, personality and character development.

Nevertheless, the mercy and grace of God was with me in all of this. God's favour was with me at all times for I never failed any of the grades. Some people made fun of me saying that I am only passing because of my age, but that was never the case. I had to work very hard for every test and exam. The truth is, I started much later with school than the other kids. They should have had an advantage, but God was with me. I always had this conviction that I had to work hard every day and push myself to be the best I could be. I did not know that I was developing some real good work ethics that serves me very well today in my workplace.

Suffering is not just bad. There are definitely some good things that can come from bad things, such as valuable life lessons and life skills. The Good Book says all things work together for our good. I have experienced this truth personally.

The best year of my time in primary school was in Grade 7. I was elected as a prefect and for the Road Patrol. This happened because there were some teachers who noticed that I had leadership abilities. Life taught me that everything happens to us is a learning curve. I was a leader in the making, although I was not really conscious of it. Leadership qualities were built into me, and today I am fulfilling a leadership role.

As an older child I had beautiful manners and leadership qualities. My Afrikaans teacher. Mr De Vries, used to call on me and one of my other friends, Wayne Arendse. We were trusted to do some other work at school and help with special projects. When I look back now, I can clearly see that I was developed to become a trusted and responsible person. These are qualities parents should develop in their children's lives. My parents did not do it, but God sent other people into my life to fulfil my parent's role.

My class teacher for that year was Mr Matthee. What a faithful man of God and what an awesome teacher! He became like a father figure to me. I remember Mr Matthee was the one who always sent me to his house to go get his wallet or money. This wonderful man trusted me and had a lot of faith in me by sending me to his home and trusting me to bring him his wallet and allowing me to take something to drink or eat when I was at his home. He was one of the greatest people I have ever encountered in my life.

Mr Matthee never judged me for being older and for not having a stable life or a decent family life. My mother and other family member moved back to Paarl at that stage of my life. My aunt took me in to stay with them and to help me finish primary school. That was a real blessing to me as a child to have people in my life who cared for me and who wanted to help me finish my primary school years.

One day Mr Matthee spoke to me and asked me what high school I would attend in 2001. I told him I had no idea, for I did not have the money to apply for any high school. My family did not have any money and my aunt were struggling financially at that time. I was not sure if I could even stay with them for another year.

Mr Matthee told me I should not worry. He would do his best to make sure I could go to high school. He spoke to my aunt and uncle to make sure I could still stay with them to finish my high school career. He also paid my registration fee at Weltevrede Senior Secondary. I owe a debt of gratitude to Newton Primary School and my class teacher, Mr Matthee. If it was not for them I would have dropped out of school with no future and no hopes.

Please invest quality time to ponder on these four powerful thoughts:
- Have the will to fight and to get up when you fall.
- Be humble. Never think that you are better than anyone else.
- Do everything with a good heart.
- Step into your destiny.

See you in Chapter 4.

Chapter 4
High school

We live life forward, but we can only understand life backwards.

In 2001 I started my high school career at Weltevrede Senior Secondary at the age of 18. For the very first time I could play rugby for the school's under 19B team. It was an awesome feeling to be part of a rugby team, even though I was the oldest guy in my class. It is indeed a wonderful thing to be accepted and approved by a team, a group or a family. A sense of belonging is a powerful and positive feeling. Psalm 68:6 says God puts the lonely in families, for God knows we are not supposed to be alone.

At last my age was no longer my worst enemy. My coach at that time was Mr Davids. He was a very supportive person. He motivated us to do our very best. He usually said, "Focus on the end goal." This phrase became my mantra that really *empowered* me on my life's journey and through many painful life experiences. What we focus on empowers us to do what we cannot do if we do not focus. Later on I discovered that successful people are very focused people.

However, things did not go smoothly in that first year in high school. My aunt and uncle experienced financial difficulties and they asked me to move back to my mother's place in Paarl. I decided not to move back to my parents since it would be too difficult for me to attend my school from their home. My parents also did not have money or transport for me to go to school from there.

After a few breakthroughs that specific day felt like the end of the world to me. I felt so hopeless and I had a terrible sense that my aunt wanted me to fail, to end up with nothing, with no hope, like all my other family members. Hurting people hurt others. They cannot help it.

The next day I told one of my friends that I have to move out of my aunt's house. He told me not to worry. Their church is holding tent services not far from our school. He invited me to come stay with them in the tent. He told me that the pastor will not mind for they needed people to stay in the tent. I welcomed this opportunity.

Again God sent me help. God is indeed a way maker. He can make a way where there seems to be no way. If we can only trust Him more to do this for us. Maybe you are experiencing some challenges now that seems impossible to overcome. Believe me, God will come through for you in his own way and time. My friend, God is our *unseen* parent. God promised to never leave us or forsake us. Make this one of your strongest positive beliefs in life. God is present in your life and He will help you in the days of trouble and in times of need. Our needs, troubles and suffering prove that God is real.

It was indeed a huge blessing for me to move into that tent. It made it possible for me to attend school each and every day. We also helped at the church and some of the church members provided us with food to eat. We helped to build the church building next to the tent. This divine opportunity caused me to meet a lot of new people and friends. I wish I knew at that time of my life that everything I went through was indeed thorough training and development. I am what I am today by the grace of God and everything I went through in life.

Those of us who stayed in the tent also took responsibility to look after the tent and all the sound equipment. Today I can look back and clearly see how God has created opportunities for me to develop a sense of responsibility. In fact, being responsible is now one of my core strengths and virtues. Responsibility means to respond positively to what life demands of you. It also means personal power. By being responsible we develop our inner power and abilities to succeed in life.

I passed Grade 8 and 9 during the two years I stayed in the church's tent. Everything was working together for my good according to the plan of God. The Good Book says God knows the thoughts and plans that He has for each one of us – thoughts and plans to prosper us and not to harm us; plans to give us a hope and a future. Hope does not disappoint.

Every day I went to school with a passion in my heart. I firmly believed that nothing is impossible for God. I was not ashamed to live in a tent. Every day was fun and at night time there were church services.

It really felt like heaven on earth for me. My heart is still filled with so much gratitude when I think or talk about those days. That season of my life has really made a great impact on me.

It also brought me happy memories, irrespective of the many years of intense suffering. This is why I am a relaxed person and easy to please. My suffering years brought out the best in me. I am so grateful about this. I can now fully understand why King David said he was glad that he was afflicted. And why Joseph said the Lord has made him fruitful in the land of his suffering. I became a fruitful and a productive human being through my suffering. All things really, really, really work together for our good.

In 2003 I started Grade 10. I was elected on the student body that year. I also became the UCSA chairperson. Life at that time was really wonderful and I was blessed to realise that other learners started seeing me as their leader. I was 20 years old at that time.

It was God's plan that I should start school at an older age. It only makes sense now.

How true is this saying, We live life toward, but we can only understand life backwards. It is only when we count our blessings one by one that we can see what God has done for us.

I did not even notice that I had become a Samuel living in the house of the Lord. I had to attend to every spiritual event, preparing the house of the Lord for services of fasting and praying every day, and living a holy life. My duties were to take care of matters pertaining to spirituality. I facilitated and coordinated worship sessions during lunch breaks in one of the classrooms. What a privilege!

Please invest quality time to ponder on these five powerful thoughts:

- You have immense power within you.
- In life, think win-win – don't think win-lose or lose-win or lose-lose.
- Consider other people, but have the courage to stand up for yourself. Let your voice be heard.
- Life rewards action – become action-oriented.
- There is so much more to life than just living and dying. Release all your potential now.

See you in Chapter 5.

Chapter 5
Releasing my potential

Good things happen to those who feel good about themselves.

My life became more positive and again I was handpicked for the rugby team. However, there was a specific year that I couldn't play rugby for the school due to my age, but I was asked to be part of the under 19 rugby teams. I was asked to motivate and inspire the teams before the games and to pray for them before every game. This too was a positive opportunity.

My life started on a destructive pathway, but little by little I shifted to a new path. Slowly but steadily I started walking on a path that would lead to success. It was really fantastic to see how the players of the first team and second team started to show me respect. Needless to say, this was a wonderful injection for my self-esteem. I started feeling good about myself. By the way, I have noticed over many years that good things follow those who feel good about themselves.

But we attract bad things when we do not feel good about ourselves and our lives.

I was a game changer for the teams because of the value I added to their lives. I started tapping into my own human potential. Later in life I realised that potential is actually *unused* power. Not one of us comes into this world without power. We don't know we are powerful because these inner powers are hidden from our eyes. However, difficult, challenging and hard times have a way of revealing these powers to us – if we think positive in negative situations and don't allow ourselves to become negative when we feel pressured. Pressure has a way of sucking different things from us. This implies that pressure reveals what we have within us. When you squeeze a lemon, it brings forth lemon juice. When a negative person is under pressure, that person will be negative. The same principle applies to a positive person.

There was a lot of people believing in me during the annual Derby Week, as I was the motivational guy of the teams and I had to put them on the field with a prayer and a few positive and empowering words. I can now clearly see that this too was a training school to develop me and lead me to motivate and inspire people. This is what I do on a daily basis now, and I hope you can see that everything we go through in life is meant to train and develop us and not to harm us, even though it does not always feel like it.

The year 2003 was also the year I had started praying the prayer of Jabez: "Lord, enlarge my territory and keep the harm away from me." The prayer of Jabez was and is considered as one of the most powerful prayers in the Good Book.

Jabez was a young boy who grew up in pain. He prayed this prayer and was radically changed and transformed. I decided to make this prayer an important part of my morning prayer time. Every morning I prayed this prayer with the utmost sincerity, determination, hope and unshakeable faith that one day something good will happen to me, just as it has happened for Jabez.

One day during break time I was asked to go to a teacher who wanted to speak to me. I nervously wondered what it was about as I walked to her classroom. She told me that another learner told her I was living in a tent not far from school. She wanted to know whether it was the truth. She could not believe it, since I am at school every day and I never looked untidy. Nor did I create any problems for any of the teachers. This was really mind blowing to her. You see, how we live really matters. You don't know who is watching you. People tend to be nice with nice people and tend to ignore people with a bad attitude. Attitude is everything!

Without any hesitation I told her the truth. I said, "Yes, Miss, I am living in a tent." She asked me how I managed to keep myself so clean every day, how I managed to keep my school uniform neat and tidy, and where I got the necessary toiletries. I told her that I do odd jobs for people and they provide me with what I need.

That day she told me that she has been praying the prayer of Jabez. I told her that I too was praying the prayer of Jabez. I think the Lord was confirming to me that it was the right thing for me to pray the Jabez prayer. It was like throwing petrol on fire. I became so much more determined to pray consistently and constantly.

This teacher told me to come around every end of the month so that she could give me money to buy toiletries. Once again I saw the hand of God working in my life. Again I saw that God is indeed an *unseen* parent. My heart was deeply touched, moved and filled with so much gratitude. I prayed, "Thank you, Lord, for your blessings upon my life." Teacher Carol Morilly was indeed a woman with a big heart for children like me. And God is blessing her for being such a person.

That same year I moved out of the tent and went to stay with a family not far from school. At last I had my own bed to sleep in. For the very first time in my life I could became part of a normal family.

The Good Book says God is a father to the fatherless. These wonderful words became so real to me. This family looked after me well and took care of all my basics needs. The goodness of God became my reality.

Please invest quality time to ponder on these four powerful thoughts:

- You are 100% responsible for your life.
- You can keep blaming someone else and remain where you are in life.
- Winners are not quitters.
- You have the ability to lead – leadership starts with leading yourself.

See you in Chapter 6.

Chapter 6
We are what we think

Most of the time, common sense is not common at all.

The year 2005 was a fabulous year and the best year of my life. I was in matric and I realised that I had indeed come far. This thought empowered me deeply. However, I was also acutely aware that I would have to work extra hard. As the saying goes, the only place where success comes before work is in the dictionary. In real life we have to work hard to obtain success.

The Good Book says God rewards diligence. Diligence means you are not afraid to put in effort and to spend energy. Many times hard work can be easy work that has been neglected. A little bit every day can make the load easier, instead of leaving everything for the last minute. It is like washing dishes. If everyone washes their plate and cup after they have eaten, there will never be dishes piling up. It is common sense. But, common sense is not so common.

I invested so much time, effort and energy to proof that I deserved to be the head boy. I never imagined that I would one day be a role model, but God ... God had other plans. I was elected as head boy in my matric year. How can I then not be a grateful person? Gratitude is the best attitude. I think gratitude keeps us humble and easy to get along with. I practise gratitude on a daily basis. In fact, I start my morning prayers with thanksgiving. The Good Book says we enter God's gates with thanksgiving.

I seriously started putting in extra study time and planned my weeks long before the exams. I told myself that I had to work harder than the rest of the learners in my class. The best way to lead is to lead by example. I intentionally listened very carefully in class to fully comprehend and understand each and every subject thoroughly. This made my study times so much easier. King Solomon said we should collect understanding. And I am reminded of the lyrics of an old song saying understanding is the best thing in the world. This is so very true.

One of my friends and I collected old examination papers and together we searched all the answers to the questions. This really helped us a lot during our study times. I remember there were people who told me I would never be able to pass matric, no matter how hard I work. Now that I think about this with a total different mind-set, I wonder if all my positive progress, that everyone could see, meant anything to them. The Good Book says let your progress be evident to everyone. This is how God gets all the glory. Potential is a gift and what we do with our potential is our gift to our Maker. Through this He shows to everyone how wonderfully He has created us. It makes God a proud father.

The best way to take revenge in a positive and healthy manner is to succeed in life. Our success humbles negative and jealous people. Their negative comments became fuel for my success. I pushed myself very hard to prove them wrong. Moreover, I carefully built all those life lessons into the foundation of my life. Unconsciously I started using my horrible life circumstances to rebuild my broken life. It is only now that I can see this clearly.

The truth is, life is a blank cheque. It's not what others write on this blank cheque that counts. It's what we write upon it with the decisions we make. That determines the outcome of our lives. We don't become what others think of us; we become what we think about ourselves. And we don't become what others say about us; what we say about ourselves makes the difference.

The Good Book says death and life lies in the power of our tongues. Yes, our words carry so much power. Power is the ability to make things happened. God did not made life complicated. We are the ones who complicate life. There is power in simplicity. Keep your life simple!

Our lives go in the direction of our most dominant thoughts. It is therefore important to make positive and empowering thoughts our most dominant thoughts. Thoughts are hidden words and words are revealed thoughts. We should develop the habit to think about what we think and be quick to reject negative and disempowering thoughts and replace them with positive and empowering thoughts.

King Solomon said, As a man thinks in his heart so is he. Can you see we are what we think and we bring about what we think? Do not forget this lesson in life.

Please invest quality time to ponder on these four powerful thoughts:
- Hard work never kills or fails.
- Laziness never brings you success.
- God helps people who work hard.
- Success is never owned.

See you in Chapter 7.

Chapter 7
The Derby and matric exams

When we feel good about ourselves, we tend to make better decisions.

The year 2005 was the year that the Derby game between Weltevrede and Bergrivier was screened live on television. For the very first time a game between non-white schools could be watched on TV. This too was a sign that things always change for the better, even though it does not always seem like it while we are going through the tough times. Change is inevitable.

On the day of the Derby they told me that the television crew will do interviews the head boy and head girl from the two schools during halftime. Wow! I will never forget that unthinkable moment. It was a jaw-dropping moment for Geduld. The poor boy from nowhere would speak on television. It still feels so unreal today, but life is full of surprises. Bad, horrible and terrible surprises, but also good and motivating surprises. God too is full of surprises, and we really need Him in our lives.

I was really blessed out of my socks. Once again I could see the hand of God working miraculously in my life. The Good Book says God is not a respecter of person, but of faith. Faith pleases God. As I said earlier, I always had faith in my heart. And here was the poor boy who used to eat from bins and landfill sites, now about to speak on national television.

The Good Book says God uses the weak things of this world to confound the strong and the foolish things of this world to confound the wise. God seems to be attracted to the outcasts and the overlooked. They are proof that God is indeed real and alive. The Good Book also says God raises the poor out of dust and lifts the needy up from the ashes.

This boy who was now about to appear on television had no choice but to wear second-hand clothes all of his broken life. But this magic moment was one of the greatest of my life. My matric year went by so very quickly. The matric farewell and exams have come and gone. And then the nerve breaking waiting period for our matric results dawned. A lot was going on in my mind.

However, I had hope. And hope never disappoints, according to the Good Book.

This thought haunted me, What would happen if I fail? What would I do? Where would I end up if I failed my matric exams? All of these questions started to bombard my mind. I could not find the stop or pause button of my busy mind.

I had many breakthroughs in life, yet I still struggled with self-doubt issues. Self-doubt is very tormenting and it causes a lack of inner peace. You always question your abilities, your sense of worth and your chances to win in life, especially if you have a background like mine. Later I learned that faith is a fight. The Good Book calls it the good fight of faith. If we continue to believe that the best is yet to come, our faith will grow stronger and overcome our doubt.

In 2006 I heard that I had passed my matric exams. But I had no future plans. As the saying goes, he who fails to plan, plan to fail. But one morning Miss Loose phoned me and she asked me, "Geduld, what are your plans for the future?" I told her I don't have any plans. She then told me to go to a college or university. This message from Miss Loose was a bright light in my dark space. My heart warmed up.

She said I should find out if there were still openings for students and to phone her back with an answer. It dawned on me again that one should have a dream or a vision for your life. Your vision is your future. No vision, no future. Life remains the same year after year when you don't have a vision for your life.

The Good Book says people perish without a vision. A vision is a mental picture of a desirable future that is much better than your current life. This conversation with Miss Loose was the beginning of my desire to create a vision for my life. I became vision conscious from that time onwards.

One can say that the best way to predict the future is to create a vision through your imagination by means of visualisation. Anyone can do this because we all have a powerful mind and an imagination. It costs no money to dream; however, money follows a dream.

Let us think a bit here. If people without a vision perish, what about people who have a vision for their lives? They tend to succeed and prosper in life. Every successful person has a vision for his or her life. This is the name of the success game.

One Tuesday morning Danielle, my best friend, and I went to Huguenot College. And we asked the big question from the woman at the enquiry counter: Were there still any openings? She sent us to Dr Lubbe. I gave her my results and she looked at them. Then she gave me forms to fill out. And, amazingly, things just started falling into place.

There is a saying in Afrikaans that became so real to me. It says, *Dinge val eers uitmekaar voordat dit in plek val.* Things always get worse before they get better. Amen!

I completed the forms and gave it to the woman at reception. Something far beyond my expectation happened during this brief moment. The woman said to me, "Welcome to Huguenot College." Wow, wow, wow! What sweet words! My life was about to change radically. She said, "You will start with a degree in Community Development next week."

Good things will and must happen when we don't give up. In consistency and persistence there is power. This power makes things happen when we tap into it through our perseverance. I am so grateful that I did not give up when I felt like giving up.

Again God showed up to show off his amazing and fabulous grace and mercy towards me. The helping hand of God miraculously pulled me into a college that never even crossed my busy mind. I was shocked because I knew nothing about a degree in Community Development, what is was all about and what it would cost me. But that is the story of the next chapter.

Please invest quality time to ponder on these four powerful thoughts:

- The number 7 in the Bible represents divine perfection. In Chapter 7 of this book my whole life changed in a positive and powerful way.
- Do you have a vision for your life? Do you have a dream? Please make time to dream, and dream big.
- This was not luck; it was the hand of God.
- In the midst of chaos, there is always opportunity. A crisis is an opportunity in disguise.

See you in Chapter 8.

Chapter 8
College

The only permanent thing in life is change.

The next day I spoke to Miss Loose about my concerns about my study expenses. She told me not to worry. She would sort out all the payments for college. I was really blessed beyond comprehension to have people like Miss Loose and her husband in my life. This is the reason why I am so determined to take nothing for granted in life. I owe a huge debt of gratitude to all the people who contributed to my life and my successes. Again God added gracious, good-hearted people to my life, just like He did over the many years.

These people made sure that all my college fees were paid on time. Miss Loose told me I just had to focus on my studies; she would handle the class fees and other money needed for my studies. Miss Loose had so much faith in me; she believed that I would make it in life. We all need people to believe in us and to show us positive things about ourselves, things we normally cannot see. We must affirm these things until we can see it. This really helped me to developed more self-confidence. The Good Book says confidence will be rewarded. This is so true.

During my college years I was a hostel leader for the private students, also in my final year. These divine opportunities schooled me further in leadership. My leadership abilities and capacities were growing fast. Today I can clearly see that life provides us many times with opportunities to grow and develop. However, we don't always see these opportunities because of the negativity in our minds. Negativity makes us blind to what is good and best for us. This is the very reason why God allows hardship and challenging situations and difficult circumstances in our lives. He sees opportunities for growth and development in all these situations. God knows what is best for us.

When we want a seed to sprout and grow, would it help to scratch open the potting soil around the seed? No, the seed will die when it gets expose to the harsh sunlight. But, when the seed sprouts in the ground and then pushes through all the obstacles under the ground, it builds strength and the capacity to handle the heat of sun and the wind and the rain. The sun and rain then become blessings to the plant. In the same way God allows us to push our way through our struggles so that we can grow strong and build capacity.

In times like this, we tend to think God has forsaken us. We think God has abandoned us when everything seems so dark. In the old days photos were developed in a dark room. Darkness brings out the best in us, even though it does not feel like it. God is more concerned about character development than comfort. Comfort and happiness is a by-product of our growth and development.

Does this make sense to you? People with a strongly developed character are normally happy people. We don't grow in a comfort zone. I also started a spiritual group as a student. The purpose and intent of the group was to help other students on campus with their spiritual growth and development. We named this group SOUT. The idea of SOUT was to have a place of safety for students from faraway places.

They could come and worship on Friday nights and have fun without any alcohol or other addictive substances. This group became like a family.

I thought a lot about this during the years. I came from a dysfunctional family, yet God chose me to build a family with the group I was working with. It is so very true that every test we go through in life becomes our testimony; our mess becomes our message, and our misery becomes our ministry. Through these experiences we can all make this sad world a better place.

Time passed so quickly. I can now see that 2008 was one of my greatest and best years on campus. I was a final-year student. I can clearly remember the call from Bonnievale I received during my final exams. I was never in this town in my whole life. A lady phoned me to ask when my exams would end for they had a job opportunity as a community development worker for me. This was another jaw-dropping life encounter for me. My future became more and more real and secure. Students normally have to do job hunting after their studies. And here I was handed a position on a platter.

I was really shocked when she told me that it was not necessary for an interview. She said I should just come to them and we could discuss an offer. What an incredible blessing from God! I did not have to go job hunting. I walked into a job after my final exams.

This experience gave me so much confidence and a bold belief that my best days were still ahead of me. The best was yet to come! I still live my life with this positive hope and expectation. You too can draw hope from my life experiences. God is not a respecter of person, but of faith. If I could develop faith in such difficult circumstances, you too can have faith.

I am becoming more and more convinced that God has allowed every bad situation and experience to happen to me for a reason. God wanted to use my life to demonstrate that He is the loving, caring, merciful, gracious and good God. This book wanted to be written. I know many educated people who are jobless and many who could not find the kind of job they have studied for. Nonetheless, things turned out very well for me, after many years of pain and suffering. No pain, no gain!

After my final exams I moved to Bonnievale and started working at Badisa. During my first year I started a group called the Badisa Kids. The idea was to have an active youth group within the community to make a difference in other people's lives. This group became very popular due to the outreach programs and school holiday programs. The Badisa head office invited me to come and speak at the Badisa general meeting. The group was asked to share their stories and the positive impact that I made on their day-to-day lives.

By the grace of God I had become a household name in Bonnievale. I became part of the community's rugby club and I was elected as chairman of Bonnievale United Rugby. This team was the top club in Bonnievale, playing in the Premier League of the South-western District. I also became the chairman of the Police Forum in Bonnievale.

After five years in Bonnievale and at the closing of our beloved offices, I moved back to

Wellington to start a new journey at a children's home. I started as a child and youth care worker looking after 15 boys in a house unit. This new beginning was really awesome and fun although also challenging. Life really became so meaningful to me. My life became purposeful and mission driven. I thank God for this. These life experiences taught me how to be a good father.

Please invest quality time to ponder on these five powerful thoughts:
- When God grants you his favour nothing can stop the blessing.
- From the fullness of his grace we have all received one blessing after another.
- God's favour outweighs and outlasts all opposition.
- God will put you at the right place at the right time.
- God will send divine connections into your life.

See you in Chapter 9.

Chapter 9
A new career

When you go through hell don't stop there. There is a better life on the other side.

One year later I was promoted to Professional Child and Youth Care Worker. The Good Book says promotion does not come from the east nor the west. God is the One who puts down one and lift up another. It was God who promoted me every time. A faithful person will abound in many blessings. There is also another saying that goes like this, If a person is faithful with little, God will make him a ruler over much.

I had to lead a team of 12 staff members and 150 kids. I was and am still mindful that my many years of suffering was God busy enlarging my inner territory and now, after so many years, my outer territory became bigger. I felt ready to take on more responsibilities. Through all my adverse circumstances I developed a sense of responsibility. For this I am indeed grateful. As with Joseph, the Lord has made me fruitful in the land of my suffering.

The promotion was really welcome. It felt like I was being rewarded for all my hard work over so many years. I was promoted after only one year at the children's home. Like Nehemiah, I could say the good hand of the Lord was upon me, for I was there only for a year before I was promoted. This means the people could see my leadership abilities and capacities. However, some people started to attack me and challenged me in my personal capacity as a leader and mentor. They tried to undermine me.

This was not a strange experience for me, because promotion always comes with persecution. And persecution, if handle positively, can lead to growth and the respect of the people who witness how you handle the attacks with a positive attitude.

During this time, I started to study again. Mr Mandela once said education is a weapon of a nation. Education can open doors that no man can shut. Education is the one thing no one can take away from you. Therefore, I beseech you, by the mercy of God, to arm yourself with education. It really does not matter how old you are. Get a decent education. People tend to respect and honour educated people. Start earning your respect.

I told myself I cannot only have a degree. I needed something more to upgrade my personal profile. So I enrolled to study Child and Youth Care and I completed my national certificate in Child and Youth Care. After finishing these studies I started with an assessor course to become a facilitator. My life journey has made me ambitious and passionate about my life calling. I had an extreme inner drive to push myself towards greater heights. I thank God for that.

I left the children home in 2016 to pursue a career in teaching and learning. One day, after a general meeting at Boland Rugby Stadium, I went with friends to Steers to eat something. At that time I had no work. I was searching for another job opportunity. As we were eating our burgers I saw a car trying to park and I walked out to warn the driver that she was about to reverse into an electric box. To my surprise it was Dr Lubbe, the same person who accepted me into Huguenot

College so many years ago. I was at the right place at the right time.

Dr Lubbe was surprised and very excited to see me. She recognised me and then asked, "What are you currently doing?" I told her I'm at home at the moment, searching for a job. She invited me to come to her office the next day and bring her my CV. She had her own private college in Bains Street in Wellington, called Cefa College.

I went there the next day and submitted my CV. The rest is history. Nothing succeeds like success. Success has a continuous rhythm and a flow once you attain your first success in life. As the saying goes, you can't keep an upbeat person down for too long. They will bounce back in due time. The Good Book also says the righteous may fall seven times, but they will rise again. Dr Lubbe was sent to my life so that I could rise again from unemployment.

My new career at Cefa College started as a teaching and learning official. This was exactly what I was studying for. God overtook me. There was a spirit of acceleration at work in my life. The

Good Book says God is able to do exceedingly and abundantly more than we could ever ask for, think or imagine beyond our wildest dreams and expectations. This new opportunity exceeded my expectations by far.

During this wonderful new season in my life I was sent all over the country to do training sessions. This was so overwhelming for me. The poor boy who went to school at the age of 10 was now flying all over the country as a training facilitator. Goodness and mercy was following me wherever I went. I was now blessed going out and blessed coming in. Is God not good!

Throughout my life I could see the hand of God upon me, beyond measure and comprehension, by day and by night. Even though the devil meant it for evil, God made it work for my good. I became the person God intended me to be. I now have a degree in Community Development, a national certificate in Child and Youth Care, and I am a highly skilled trained assessor and facilitator with a job in local government where I see so many young people with a good and positive stories to tell.

This is what makes my life so meaningful. These young people do not have to go through all the painful life experiences that I had to go through year after year. Nonetheless, there is a promise land after every wilderness or season of suffering. Every great person in this world has a sad story to tell. But better days lie ahead of all of us.

I would like to encourage everyone reading this book with the following words: *The only time we fail is when we stop trying.* Keep going. That is all you can do. And if you fail, fail forward. To fail is a first attempt in learning. There is hope for the hopeless. The Good Book says hope does not disappoint because the love of God has been shed in our hearts by the Holy Spirit who was given to us.

Our history is His Story. God wants your life to tell a story to help many people and to make this world a better place for all of his people. There is a *calling* for all of us to become Change Agents and Game Changers.

Please invest quality time to ponder on these four powerful thoughts:

- The favour that you ask, shows spirit and interventions.
- Other people may have more talents, higher education or more valuable experience, but God's favour can cause you to go places.
- When God chooses you, it really doesn't matter who else has rejected or neglected you.
- Favour increases and enhances blessings.

See you in Chapter 10 to conclude my life story.

Chapter 10
Become a blessing

Be determined to become a Change Agent or a Game Changer.

We all came into this world for a reason, to fulfil a purpose and an assignment. We can either live to impress people or to impact people. An impression lasts for a brief moment, but an impact can have an everlasting effect on society, on the world, on the life of one person or on a nation. We grow and expand step by step and little by little from our own family life, gaining community influence, locally, nationally, international and ultimate globally.

Where are you now, and where do you intend to go in life?
As you journeyed with me through the chapters and pages of this book you might have noticed that I was very open, honest and transparent about my life with all its painful, shameful and terrible life experiences. Freedom is found in hiding nothing. It's bondage to carry around secrets. Your secrets give the devil power over

your life. Secrets create darkness in us and the devil is king over darkness.

No one in this world is exempt from trouble. Jesus clearly said in this world we shall have trouble, but be of good sheer, for Jesus came to overcome the world. Through Jesus' victory we can have victory in this world. His victory overcomes the world.

Sadly, some of us hide negative, bad or shameful things about ourselves. We prefer to pretend or wear a mask to create a good impression before others. Personality is who you are in the light where everyone can see you, but character is who you are in the dark where no one can see you.
Who are you really?

Let's be clear about this, for there are people waiting to hear your sad story to give them a sense of hope to overcome their own sad story. Every great man or woman has a sad story to tell. When it comes to playing the cards, you cannot determine whether your hand of cards will be easy or difficult to play. You just have to do your very best with the cards that was handed to you.

Life has handed me very difficult cards to play. When we have difficult cards we sometimes have to skip rounds and this put us behind others. How many rounds have I skipped when I only went to school at the age of 10! Although I was behind everyone, it is interesting to note that I ended up first many times.

I got promoted instead of people who worked years longer than I have. I did not have to seek for a job. The boy who was last many times in his life came first. The Good Book says the first shall be last and the last shall be first. This is what you have seen as you were reading my sad life story. My story is now bringing glory to God.

Let's go back to playing cards. There is no real thrill when you win with easy cards. This is because you had a head start. However, if you have difficult cards to play, you will feel far more satisfied and fulfilled when you win.

My friend, whatever type of life you have to live does not make you a good or a bad person. On the contrary, you were a victim and maybe your parents were victims too. We cannot give what we don't have. Therefore, your life was a bad consequence due to the previous generation. You are not to be blamed; you don't have to feel ashamed or condemned. Nor should you allow other people to put you on a guilt trip. Shake off the shame, the condemnation and the guilt; lift up your head. Walk boldly and be determined to play your difficult cards wisely and thoughtfully.

Can you do this? Yes, you can! Just do it and win big time. Many rich and wealthy people were born in poverty, but they chose to rise above those challenging circumstances. You can do the same. The only difference between you and being a game changer is you!

We read about Joseph in the Good Book. He was thrown in a well and sold by his brothers; he was thrown into prison innocently. This man played his difficult cards wisely and got promoted in jail and later on became second in charge of Egypt, the most powerful nation then.

Nelson Mandela was thrown in jail for 27 years and became the first black president in South Africa. This has paved the way for Barack Obama to become the first black president of the USA. What about Oprah Winfrey? She grew up in poverty and was molested by her uncle. She became one of the richest and influencing black women in the entire world.

And what about Geduld? He went through so much pain and suffering and ended up working for the government.

The Good Book says the God of mercy comforts us during our trials and tribulations so that we can comfort others with the same comfort that we have been comforted with. God wants to comfort you in your hardship, but you have to ask Him to comfort you. It is written, You do not have, because you do not ask. Another verse says, Ask and you will receive.

When we receive comfort from the Lord we will become a source of comfort for others and lead them through their troubled times. This is a precious and wonderful gift and ability to have such powers to help, assist, support and empower people. He who waters others, shall also be watered. We will become better and stronger when we serve other people.

Jesus said whosoever serves others will become great in this world. Mandela once said playing small does not benefit anyone. He then said, please become great so that others can benefit from your life. Let me repeat: We can only give what we have. Of what benefit will we be to others if we did not have to go through trials, tribulations, hardships, suffering and pain? What life lessons do you gain from living a comfortable and easy life?

Let's go and grow through whatever we have to go through in life. It's not enough to go through things; we must *grow* through what we *go* through. Let us stop being negative and start seeking for something positive in our situations. There is always something positive in anything that is negative, and it is possible to be positive in any negative situation. We have the power to choose. We can choose to be negative or positive.

There is no power stronger than the power to choose. No one and nothing can make you do something that you choose not to do. The more we tap into our power to choose, the stronger and more powerful will we become. You are far more powerful than you know. There is a power in you that you have not yet used.

However, we give our power away when we blame or accuse others, when we murmur, complain, make excuses and become negative about things. These things then start controlling us with the power we have given away.

I was surrounded with so many reasons to complain, murmur, become negative and blame and accuse others. If I gave in, I would never have been where I am today, by the grace of God.

In conclusion, you went through a lot in life. Don't waste your experiences. Find a way to share your life's experiences with the people who need help, assistance and support. Making a contribution is a powerful thing. It produces a sense of satisfaction, fulfilment and happiness. Jesus said it is better to give than to receive. Giving empowers the giver. The Good Book says, Give and it shall be given you.

Take a pen and a book. Spend at least 30 minutes to an hour every day thinking about your life journey. Start writing down all the life lessons that you have learned through your trails, tribulations and hardships. Don't think too hard. Writing is a flow. Just go with the flow. There is life in the flow. And remember, we live life forward, but we can only understand life backwards.

Look back and you will see why you had to go through certain things that were painful at that time. You are a different person now. You have more knowledge and you are wiser. You will make sense of the things you could not previously understand.

The information in this book is a treasure and riches that you can share with others. It will motivate, bless, encourage, comfort, inspire and bring hope to the hopeless. It will empower many. Pray over this book and ask God to bless what He has given you over many years. Finally, ask God to show you how to use what you have received, and to provide you with open doors and opportunities to help many people.

The lowest place in God's kingdom is to be blessed. The highest place is to be a blessing. Become a blessing.

Please invest quality time to ponder on these closing powerful thoughts:
- In one season David was a shepherd; in the next season he was a king.
- In the one season Ruth was working in the field; in the next season she owned the same field.
- In one season Mordechai was sitting outside the king's palace; in the next season he was inside the palace.
- The God who turns things around is the God of unmerited favour.
- God's favour follows me everywhere I go.
- Psalm 23:6 says, "Surely goodness and mercy shall follow me all the days of my life; and I will dwell in the house of the Lord forever."

I really hope you have enjoyed this journey with me.

Love and grace
Geduld

Bible references

Chapter 1
1. Ephesians 3:20
2. 1 Corinthians 13:14

Chapter 2
1. Mark 9:23
2. John 6:35

Chapter 3
1. Proverbs 19:17
2. Philippians 4:12
3. Isaiah 41:10
4. Hebrews 4:16

Chapter 4
1. Psalm 103:13
2. Psalm 46:1
3. Jeremiah 29:11
4. Psalm 119:71
5. Genesis 41:52

Chapter 5
1. Chronicles 4:10
2. Psalm 68:5-6
3. Psalm 145:9

Chapter 6
1. Proverbs 10:4
2. Psalm 100:4
3. 1 Timothy 4:15
4. Proverbs 23:7

Chapter 7
1. Acts 10:34
2. 1 Corinthians 1:27
3. Proverbs 29:18

Chapter 9
1. Psalm 75:6
2. Matthew 25:23
3. Romans 5:5

Chapter 10
1. Matthew 19:30
2. Genesis 37:24
3. 2 Corinthians 1:4
4. Luke 6:38

www.ingramcontent.com/pod-product-compliance
Lightning Source LLC
Chambersburg PA
CBHW051433090426
42737CB00014B/2947